爸爸媽媽，
請你看見我！

Dad and Mom, please see me!

蔡沅達 著

目錄 CONTENTS

Chapter 1

序言與專訪

FOREWORD & INTERVIEW

01.Dr. Chen 的話

陳總顧問

回憶是一道又一道的門。總是有人說著小時候好多的記憶都忘了，彷彿那一段最為寶貴兒時成長的過程被關閉起來，它慢慢的如同關了一扇又一扇的窗，心門卻不知不覺隨著那道門、那扇窗也關閉了。

且讓時空回到 2017 年，那是在一個舉世聞名，小而精、而美的綠色城市新加坡，就像偶遇相見的機緣認識，蔡沅達是個 15 歲男孩，那是充滿著靦腆、純真、善良面容，眼睛大大的，卻布滿了血絲，講話時，有一種好理直氣壯的樣貌。當一開口就說：「我好累哦！」突然間，讓我覺得更有一股累積好久且強大被壓抑的憤怒能量無法釋放出來。這個孩子怎麼了？怎麼會！有這樣極大反差呢？

在過去 20 幾年從事許多青少年輔導工作的經驗，在他的背後一定經歷很多不容易的事件發生，或者是一種故事的延伸。蔡沅達 3 歲時，爸媽就因著性格不合而離異，媽媽個性是剛硬強勢的女人，爸爸是相當

有感性平和的男人。孩子啊！那心中的第一道門也就關起來了，就像把自己關進去一層又一層暗黑無比的象牙塔內，禁錮著這麼靦腆、純真、純善、純美的孩子靈魂啊！

時間快速拉回 2021 年的現在時刻，我正注視看著沅達這本畫作冊初稿。沅達是獨子，沒有其他兄弟姐妹，爸媽離異後，與爸爸同住一起，所幸媽媽仍有一直陪伴著。無論如何？大人感情世界到底是怎樣呢？怎麼可以這樣呢？那我呢？

光陰似箭，歲月如梭，日子卻以十分漫長且很慢地圍繞著這孩子。想到學校讀書，卻遇到了人際關係的阻礙及衝突，「我再次壓抑憤怒不已的自己」「沒有人可以再霸凌我」，網路世界是可以幫助我重建這個世界的。彷彿新的概念、認知、觀點一個個被點燃了。2017 年終於為自己打開第一扇門了。

「陳主任」「陳老師」「Dr. Chen」哈哈哈！其實與大家分享，至今沅達從未這樣在我面前稱呼過，但孩子卻十分清楚知道我是誰哦！「內心藏著 5 個不一樣的他」是孩子不經意具體透露出來的，他想著應該要好好面對及整合自己的時刻到了，尤其孩子總是怒目

口頭禪說著：「媽媽很笨！」原來這一切都是愛的保護！從小恐懼自己被霸凌，更害怕媽媽被欺負啊！外面環境的陌生人也不安全呀！

　　不知覺與這畫作冊名稱《爸爸媽媽，請你看見我！》有了更深度的意識連接，它帶入到「當我 20 歲，爸媽就沒事了」。孩子正一直在蛻變整合著自己呢，就像毛毛蟲準備破繭而出，轉化為彩蝶啊！那是孩子給自己最強大的期許及未來希望啊！「20 歲的我！我長大成熟了！我可以開始展翅飛翔！爸媽你們不須要再為我擔心著了！」

　　再專注看著沅達所創作 19 幅畫作，這是在 2019 年因著「家油站」開幕誌慶，孩子很貼心的念頭觸機畫了幾幅做為贊助義賣所延續擴展而來的。以下概分為五大系列，有「系列一：感受」「系列二：大洞」「系列三：通道」「系列四：悲傷之路」「系列五：幸福之路」，尤其是每一系列裡更蘊藏著此畫作者對自屬生命無盡的感受及深刻體認。

　　例如：1 感受：是傾聽自己的聲音；2 大洞：是向內遇見黑暗與恐懼；3 通道：是心靈通道，生命的拐點；4 悲傷之路：是穿越幽暗重新聚足力量；5 幸福之路：是連接無限可能。到底沅達畫作者究竟欲想藉由此 19 幅作品，帶領我們大人進入怎樣的世界，那麼，就讓大家好好的以輕鬆愉悅的態度進入孩子內心世界探索而知。

　　最後！我以大人的身分及角色，再次分享：孩子一直都是我們最棒的生命禮物，他們就像一面清澈明亮的鏡子照耀著，期盼讓大人們也能從中窺見些什麼？

　　就在此時此刻傳來內在訊息，我想告訴孩子啊！「親愛的沅達，你是最棒的！」

2021.08.09　筆於臺灣立秋時分

01. Foreword

by Dr.Chen － Consultant Chen

Memories are like a series of doors, one after another. There are bound to have some who proclaimed that they have forgotten most of their childhood memories, as if that precious piece of growing up process were being shut off. It is like slowly shutting off the windows, one by one. The door to the heart also unknowingly followed the doors and windows in shutting off.

Allow time to return to 2017, a world famous, small and refine, beautiful and green city [Singapore], where a chance encounter met a chance acquaintance. [Taro Chua] was a 15 year old boy, shy, innocent and kind. His eyes were big but were bloodshot, and he was straightforward in his speech. At the moment when he first blurted out: "I am so tired!", I felt that there was a huge and long accumulated ounce of energy in him, suppressed by rage and no way to release.

What happened to this boy? How can the contrast be so drastic?

From my past 20 over years of experience in youth counselling, I reckon that he must have experienced some matters of grave difficulties or an extension of a story of the same. [Taro Chua], his parents divorced due to incompatibility when he was 3 years old. The mother was a strong headed woman whereas the father was more sensible and gentle. Oh, child! There goes to the shutting of the first door to the heart as if you have caged yourself in the darkest levels of the ivory tower, imprisoning the shy, genuine, kind - hearted and beautiful pure soul of a child.

Fast forward the time to the present year 2021, I am looking at the first draft of [Taro]'s album. Taro is the only child without any siblings. He lived with his dad after the parents' divorce, and fortunately, his mom was always there for him.

Whatever it is? What is in the adult's emotional world? How can it be in this way? What about me? Time flies like an arrow, age is like a shuttle, but the days surrounding this child were long and slow. The drive to go and learn in school was obstructed by the conflict and unfriendly environment.

"Once more, I suppressed the rage in me. " "Nobody can ever bully me again".

The internet world is able to help me to reconstruct this world, as if this new concept, knowledge and point of view were being ignited one by one. In 2017, he opened the first door, for himself.

"HOD Chen" "Teacher Chen" "Dr Chen" Hahaha! Just to share with you, although

Taro has never addressed me with any of the aforesaid titles, he is very sure [who I am!]

[The hidden 5 different identities in his inner world] was not easily revealed by him. He reckon that it was time for him to address and integrate himself. Particularly, the child's angry look together with his mantra of "Mother is so stupid!" was in fact a form of protection out of love. He was afraid of being bullied since young, hence was even more fearful for his mom being bullied!

Strangers from the external environment were not safe also. Hence unknowingly the name of the album [Dad and Mom, please see me!] has gained deeper connection to the consciousness. It then brought about [my parents will be okay when I turned 20]. The child is in the midst of continuous transformation and integration! Just like the caterpillar ready to break free from its cocoon to become a colourful butterfly! That is the strongest anticipation and hope of the future the child has granted himself. The 20 year old me! I have grown and am mature. I can start to spread my wings and soar! Dad and mom, you need not worry about me anymore!

Refocusing on Taro's album of 19 art pieces, this is the resulting fusion of a caring child's sponsorship of a few art pieces for charity sales during the opening ceremony of [Sumari Sage Tree - Jia You Zhan]. The series are as follows: [series 1: Feeling], [series 2: Big Hole], [Series 3: Path], [Series 4: Sadness Path] and [Series 5: Happiness Path].

More in particular, each series contains the author's feelings towards the infinity of life and deep realization.

For example,

1. Feeling: Listening to your inner voice

2. Big Hole: Encountering the darkness and fear

3. Path: Passage of the soul, turning point of life

4. Sadness Path: Traversing the darkness, regathering of power

5. Happiness Path: Connecting to infinite possibilities

In this album of 19 art pieces, what kind of world does the author Taro wants to lead us adults into? Let us discover by relaxing ourselves and enter into the inner world of a child with joy.

Lastly, I want to share again, as a role of an adult, children has always been the best gift in life. They are as clear as a sparkling mirror, anticipating what we adult can glimpse from it.

At this juncture came a message from within, I wish to tell the child: Dear Taro, you are the best!"

Penned on 9th August 2021, Beginning of Autumn, Taiwan

02. 輔導與心理治療師的話

郭素珍

「聆聽……聆聽……聆聽孩子的『心聲』……敞開那一扇又一扇為你等待的門……」

真心感謝陳志成總顧問的引導，並且允許身為母親和心理輔導治療師的我，一起全程參與此畫冊的製作過程。這段歷程帶領我潛入了一段深入的潛意識海洋探索之旅。

很難想像發生在我自己身上，從 2017 年的我未曾接受任何醫療，乳房硬塊的自我療癒，沅達畫冊創作及身心狀態的自我整合過程，陳總顧問看似個別性引導，但卻能啟動整個家庭（其實是兩個家族）的核心心靈動力，這是心理學，甚至輔導或心理治療所不會，或很難達到的一種相對性心靈動力，一次又一次讓我親身體驗也見證了他的輔導陪伴，實在是奇蹟般的超越傳統心理學，竟是如此的究竟！

我心中想給天下所有的父母一個最為基本的提問：「到底是孩子怎麼了？」還是根本是「我們大人到底怎麼了？」

此畫冊的作者蔡沅達表達出許多孩子的心境：內心有最想跟大人說，卻說不出口的話；無法對大人說出自己最真實的感受，甚至想法；在大人面前，無法如實展現自己的真正潛能；看見大人赤裸裸的真相，卻又貼心的選擇讓自己「笨」的方式來默默等待，等待有一天大人的陪伴……這些「不說的」或「說不出口的」真的是說不出口嗎？恰恰相反，那是份給予父母最單純無私的愛呀！說穿了，是顧忌父母內心的感受啊！

最為核心的是沅達媽媽「聽見」孩子了，願意臣服，忠實且誠正的覺察與觀照、面對自己，慢下來陪伴彼此學習，一起從扭曲混亂裡走出去。

18 歲的沅達真的是個智者。他的靈視世界觀竟是如此宏觀、通透大人的世界，就好像我在為他做訪談的翻譯時，他卻像是在看戲的觀察者，等著看看大人如何採訪他，而不是他被觀察，乖乖的等著接受採訪。這畫冊呈現了沅達對於生命的存在感、主觀感受表達的勇氣和力道，是一般孩子很難做到的，對比於大人的內心世界反卻是充滿恐懼、狹隘和保守。

此畫冊想傳遞給所有讀者「希望」和「聆聽孩子（的心聲）」，允許彼此以「主觀感受表達」來建立「溝通的橋梁」。

此畫冊的每一幅畫都是沅達真實穿越的成長歷程，傳達著最大的鼓勵和生命的無限可能。我深深的祝福每一位讀者：在你們耐心閱讀的同時，也能從中找到屬於每一個人內心的那扇門。這本畫冊就是旋開你心中「門把手」的勇氣──讓你能敞開那一扇又一扇為你等待的門。

02.Foreword

by Vanessa Keh - Counsellor & Psychotherapist

Listen… Listen… Listen to your child's "Inner Voice"… . Open the doors that is waiting for you… .

I sincerely thank Consultant, Mr Chen ZhiCheng (Dr Chen), for his guidance and allowing me, as a mother and Counsellor & Psychotherapist, to participate and work together in the production process of this Art Expression Album. This journey has led me to an amazing exploration - a deep dive into the ocean of subconsciousness.

Never have I thought that this could happen to me. From my hardened breast lumps which was not medically treated since 2017, to self-healing; from Taro's Art Expression Album and his self - integration process; Consultant Chen's

爸爸媽媽，
請你看見我！

Dad.and Mom, please see me!

蔡沅達 著

目錄 CONTENTS

guidance may seem to be for individual, but it could actually ignite the entire family's (in fact two families clan) core psyche-dynamics. I have personally experienced and witnessed numerous times of Dr Chen's counselling companionship, this relative psyche-dynamics which cannot or perhaps maybe difficult for any psychology, counselling and/or psychotherapy to achieve, and definitely is miraculous surpassing conventional psychology.

From the deepest of my heart, I would like to suggest to all the parents in the world the most basic question: "Is it about our child?" or "more precisely, is it about us, the adult?"

Taro Chua, the author of this Art Expression Album, helps express and exhibit the inner world of many children and adolescents: The things that they most wanted to say to the adults yet cannot say it out; the truest feelings/emotions that they cannot genuinely express nor even their thoughts to the adults; and the innate potentials that they cannot display in front of the adults. They are able to see the whole naked truth about the adults world yet thoughtfully chose to behave "stupid" just to wait silently hoping for the company of the adults… . Is it really that these "unspoken words" or "inexpressible words" cannot be spoken? On the contrary, towards the parents - They are showing their most simple, unselfish, and unconditional love! The truth is, they mind too much about their parents' feelings!

Most importantly, Taro's mother "hears" him. She is willing to surrender, be honest and truthful to reflect and face herself, slowing down her pace to learn with Taro, so as to walk out of the distortion and chaos together.

18-year-old Taro, is really a wise man, like a Sage. The adult world is as transparent as a glass in his macroscopic psyche worldview. Just

like while I am interpreting the interview for him, he was more like an observer watching a play, and waiting to see how we will interview him rather than obediently waiting to be interviewed. This Art Expression Album displayed Taro's courage and strength towards his sense of life's existence and subjective feeling expression which may not be as easy for any other children or adolescents. In comparison, the adult world perhaps is usually full of fear, narrowness and conservative.

This Art Expression Album hopes to deliver to all the readers: To deliver "Hope" and "listen - listen to the voices of your child", and to allow one another to "express their feelings subjectively" so as to build the [bridge of communication].

Every of Taro's art piece in this album is a benchmark on his growth and development process that convey an inspirational infinite possibility of life. With my heart, I sincerely wish every reader: Be patience while reading this Art Expression Album, so that you may find the inner door that belongs to your heart. This Art Expression Album represents courage, the key for you to turn the "door-knob" opening to all the doors and beyond that's waiting for you in your heart.

03. 媽媽的話

郭素珍

「你就像夜空中最亮的星（心），照亮著我前行，看見生存的意義……我有個『我們』……」

相信每一位母親都很想走入孩子的內心世界，想知道到底該如何懂得孩子要的是什麼？想知道到底如何讓孩子知道我們所做的都是為他好。我也是這樣「住進」了一套又一套的外衣（身分）， 被這些許多的期待、壓力、面子、愧疚和無助框架、綁架了自己。

2017 年，Dr.Chen 送了我一句「為母則強」。經由此話的力量和其無比耐心、細膩的引導陪伴下，2019 年，啟動了整個畫冊創作歷程迄今。身為母親的我參與了整個過程，從第一次的畫展開始，的確很不容易。無數次的心酸、心疼、淚水，因而大哭著……需要相當深的忠實且誠正的自我面對。 這樣的「不容易」不單單只是面對自己最黑暗的一面而已，也包含需要內在的勇氣面對「看見孩子心理的傷疤」，如同沅達透由系列五的《諒解》作品告訴了我：「媽媽，請妳把心中的那把鎖打開，面對妳自己，才能看見我呀！」

在此，感謝我的孩子沅達，你沒有放棄我，讓我上了非常珍貴的一堂課！學會懂得如何成為一個孩子的母親，也讓我面對了過去身為你的爸爸的妻子，懂得如何真正成為人妻。是你讓我相信自己是值得被愛的，讓我也能夠成為真實的自己。你是如此深愛著我和爸爸，你的貼心讓我好感動、好感動……沅達，你是媽媽的驕傲！我也要謝謝沅達的爸爸，辛苦你了！

此書冊更同時啟動了我的原生家庭心靈動力，轉化了沅達的外婆，放下了對孩子所有的擔心，回到了信任，因為孩子長大了。相對的，沅達的外婆、我的媽媽，也面對了她的過去，給予現在的我們更多關懷和溫暖的愛。

我也要感謝所有參與此書冊出版的團隊（蘇馬利體集團）和我們全家人的老師、導師——陳志成總顧問耐心細心的引導。

我想對孩子沅達說：「你就像那夜空中最閃亮的一顆星，是你的光，照亮了，也推動了我重拾前進的力量、看見生命最可貴的存在意義……是你， 讓我有個『我們』……」

■ 郭素珍 Vanessa Keh

BABM(Hons)
Counsellor & Psychotherapist(APACS)
工商管理學士 (榮譽)
輔導與心理治療師 (新加坡心理治療師和輔導員協會)
簡歷：
一位擁有工商管理（榮譽）學位和社會心理學與輔導學文
憑的企業家，也是作者蔡沅達的母親。
目前攻讀輔導與心理治療師的碩士學位。
她支持企業精神、熱愛自然、旅行、娛樂和閱讀。希望透
過學習，激發出每個人的潛能與力量，以愛和完成自我價
值來創造自己的實相。

03.Foreword

by Vanessa Keh - Taro's Mother

You are like the brightest star (heart) illuminating me as I move forward and see the meaning of existence... I have "US"...

I believe every mother would want to path into the inner world of our child, would like to know how we could understand what our child needs… would like to know how to make our child understand what we are doing is all for their best. With Such, I let myself "lived" in the many different sets of coats (identities), and was kidnapped by these frames of expectations, peer pressures, face values, guilt and helplessness.

In 2017, Consultant Chen (Dr. Chen) bestowed me with a statement - "A Mother's Strength". With the power of this statement, and his great patience and delicate guidance, the creation of this Art Expression Album started in 2019.

I thank my child, Taro, for not giving up on me and gave me a very precious lesson instead! I learned to truly understand how to become a mother for a child, that allows me to face my past as a wife, and to understand how to become a wife for a husband. You make me believe that I am worthy of love so that I can genuinely be my authentic self. I am so touched and moved by your delicateness and sensitivity with your love for your father and I, seems so deep. Taro, you are my pride, and I am proud of you! I also want to thank Taro's father as it wasn't any easy on him too!

This Art Expression Album concurrently vastly ignited the psyche-dynamics of my origin family that transformed Taro's grandmother to let go of all her worries for her children. By returning to trust - She recognized her children has finally grown up. Relatively, Taro's grandmother who is my mother, subtly addressed her own past experiences. Thus, giving us now, much more of her care, warmth, and love.

Special thanks to the whole team from SUMARI GROUP and all the people who participated and involved in this Art Expression publication. I want to thank especially to Consultant Chen (Dr Chen), for being my whole family's Teacher and Mentor; no words could ever express our deepest appreciation to his extremely patience and delicate guidance rendered to us.

I want to tell my child, Taro: "You are the brightest star in the night sky. It is your light that illuminated me and regained my strength to move forward, and see the most precious meaning of life⋯

It is you who had given "US"⋯

04. 諮商心理師的話

呂仁捷

生活像是個不斷重複的循環，透過打開一扇門，穿越過幽暗的隧道，光就在那。

與沅達互動的過程一下感覺他是個智者，常講一些深奧的道理，面對 18 歲的臉孔不免讚嘆又感慨；一下感覺他是個調皮的小孩，把一堆哥哥姊姊繞得團團轉；一下表情嚴肅，肅殺氣氛的背後有顆疲倦的心，讓我不禁隔著螢幕用眼神努力傳達溫暖的擁抱，但互動過程中，沅達大多時候是個爽朗、愛笑的大男孩，大方分享著自己創作的歷程與背後想要傳達的理念。

對於非美術相關科系出身的我來說，第一眼看到畫作最主要的感受就是困惑，有幸透過專訪，聽見沅達的生命歷程與創作理念，彷彿看見畫作打開了一道「門」，走進了畫作的深度，看見不同的風景與意象。

從跟疼痛有關的畫作中，看見沅達展現了過往所面對的苦痛，像是在黑暗中迷了路，不斷繞圈子的孩子，加上敏感細膩的特質，身旁的冷漠與攻擊都成了一道道刻在心裡的傷痕，也許正是因著這些經驗，讓沅達打磨出令人讚嘆的勇氣與明白。這份勇氣讓沅達足以往內探索，打開一道道內心的房門，與充滿遺憾、憤怒、難過的自己和解。明白則帶領沅達向外開展，能了解自己的目標，也能理解與尊重他人的不同立場，而能率真的開創生命的精彩，能有這樣的轉變，其中很重要的是「門」的概念。

沅達把門比喻為終結循環的突破點，當我們找到了門，就像是不斷循環的生命有了新的可能性，站在門前也許有些期待與害怕，但從畫作中感受到最多的是生命得以不同的希望感，而貼心的沅達也將開門的選擇權交到每一位讀者的手中。很像在諮商過程，個案已經找到了那扇關鍵的大門，常因擔心、害怕而在門前躊躇不前，即便諮商師再急、再心疼個案，還是得將開門的權利交給個案，因只有自己轉動門把踏出去，才不容易又回到原本的循環，期待讀者可以透過沅達的畫作，連結到內心的一扇門，勇敢且自在地開啟生命不同可能。

沅達還有一部分的畫作讓我感受到滿滿的溫暖，傳達了人與人的情感連結，與孩子對於玩耍的期待，沅達也直接地說，希望提醒看到畫作的父母們，可以因此多陪陪孩子，創造一些難忘的童年與歡樂。這本畫冊從疼痛的經驗出發，連結到希望感、可能性與創造力，最後再以倡議的方式表達遺憾的經驗，看見沅達將這份疼痛轉化為愛流動到每位讀者的心中。期待讀者閱讀過程中也能給自己一點時間，在每一幅畫作前面停留與連結，或許就不小心連結到一扇門，而開啟了嶄新的生命體驗。

📑 呂仁捷

中山醫學大學 心理系
國立臺中教育大學 諮商與應用心理學系 碩士班
簡歷：
賽斯教育基金會（青年團總召／網路資訊部部長）
失親兒福利基金會（社工員）
心生活協會（IMR 康復服務 - 專業服務員）

04.Foreword

Foreword by Lu Renjie － Psychologist

Life is like endless vicious cycle, by opening a door, and passing through the dark tunnel, light is there.

I felt Taro is a wise man during our interaction as he spoke profound truth like a sage. Looking at the face of a 18 year old, I was filled with admiration and lament. At a moment, he was like a mischievous kid who made a group of elder brothers and sisters spinning in circles. The next moment, his facial expression was stern but a tired heart that lies behind all seriousness. I can't help but sending him warm psychological hugs through my eyes via the screen; nonetheless, during most of the interaction, Taro likes to laugh like a candid big boy. He generously shared about his journey of his own creation unreservedly to convey his underlying ideology.

For a non - art student like me, I felt perplexed when I first saw the Art Expression work. Fortunately, through this interview, I get to hear about his life journey and the idea behind his creation. It was as if seeing the art piece opens up a door, and went deeper into the Art Expression work to see the different scenery and images.

From the related [Pain] in the Art Expression series, I saw Taro's expression of his pain in the past, just like being lost in the darkness and kept going round in circles. Due to his unique trait of sensitivity and exquisiteness, the indifferences and defences around him etched scars in his heart. It could be due to this experience that Taro was able to develop admirable courage and understanding. The courage was enough to lead Taro to self-discovery by opening up the doors

in his heart and make peace with his regrets, rage and sadness; the understandings led Taro to open outwardly to understand his own objective, and to understand and respect others with different perspectives. This enables Taro to honestly and truthfully create the splendour in his life. The "door" is one of the most important concept for such a transformation to happen.

Taro used doors as an example of the ultimate breakthrough point to stop the vicious cycle. When we discover a door, it is like discovering a new possibility to the vicious cycle of life. Standing in front of the door, one may anticipate hope and fear, but what one can feel most from the Art Expression work is that life can be of different sense of hope. Taro delicately pass the choice of opening the doors to all the readers. This is just like in my practice where my client discovered the key significant door but due to his/her worry and fear, he/she just stay still squatting in front of the door. No matter how anxious and sorry I may feel for my client, I have to pass the choice of opening the doors to them. Only when one turns the door knob and stepped out themselves, they will then not fall back into the vicious cycle. I sincerely hope that through Taro's Art Expression Album, readers are able to connect the door in their heart, spontaneously and bravely ignite the different possibilities in life.

There is some part in Taro's Art Expression work that gave me enormous warmth as it conveyed the connections about inter - relationships. With regards to children's expectation during their playtime, Taro directly said that he hopes to remind parents who sees his Art Expression Album, can spend more time with their children to create a fonder and happy childhood memories for them.

[Pain] is the outset of this Art Expression Album that connects sense of hope, possibilities and creativity, and lastly to initiate the expression of regretful experiences, it is obvious that Taro had transformed pain into love which will flood into the hearts of all readers. I look forward to all the readers to give yourself some time, stay a little longer to connect with each art piece, and perhaps you may connect to one of the door which may open up a whole new life experience.

05. 專訪

陳心怡

▇█ 序幕 █▇

　　蔡沅達，2021 年滿 18 歲，和時下年輕人並無二致，喜歡動漫、電玩、計算機科學，思考跳耀，表達真誠，毫不造作。談到內心深處時，整個人投入表達的力道是竭盡所能地讓你知道並理解他所有的想法。

　　多年前，他曾被精神科醫生診斷為社交隔離症狀，也就是一種比較傾向脫離現實感的情形。這標籤一貼上去，被心靈大地震撞擊的不只是沅達，還有母親郭素珍、父親蔡俊鵬；也幾乎在同一時間，沅達無心的隨手畫，被大人看見了。畫畫，其實早已默默的在沅達的生命中陪伴他度過無數的無聊、無力、憤怒，甚至是痛不欲生的迷惘童年，只是忙碌的大人從不知道他的祕密世界。童年的他，對於生命已經有了很大的問號。人，究竟為何而活？

　　在沅達口中的「Dr. Chen」──陳志成老師的鼓勵下，他把內心世界一幅一幅畫了下來。他一路用自己的生命探尋答案，身痛、心痛，午夜夢迴不知經歷千百次瀕臨滅頂的痛，這孩子究竟想要吶喊些什麼？想要告訴大人什麼？

　　這次採訪不是項容易的任務。語言使用是其一，沅達的思維邏輯往往是多方平行，若追不上，就很難理解他的心；其次，聰明的他，常常會用一種看戲的心，想看看大人如我，究竟要如何與他對話。為了能夠更貼近他的內心，我們採訪了三次，兩次是在午夜時分。夜深，總容易有更多的真實的聲音冒出來呈現內在的自己。

▇█ part 1：6/25(五) 17:30 2 小時 █▇

　　事後回看第一次採訪，才明白這只是個暖身與開場，雖然採訪時間延續了兩個小時之久，但多半是在熟悉沅達的特質與表達方式。沅達善用英語表達，必須仰賴素珍翻譯，因此在採訪過程中，「母親」的參與是一種特別的橋梁。素珍原汁原味翻譯沅達所說以及我的提問，不帶任何母親的色彩做為濾鏡，沒讓翻譯加上母親的調料而失真。

　　沅達不只一次用「笨蛋」形容自己，也把媽媽扯進來：「我就是一個笨蛋，我是一個笨蛋媽媽的孩子。」

但他對於媽媽的陪伴是心知肚明的，還問我：「妳要聽媽媽的故事嗎？這個媽媽，我可以講她的故事講到她會哭，妳們也會哭。」一般父母親聽到孩子這樣向外人表達，不一定受得了，而素珍不僅穩穩的聽，甚至，她對於兒子能夠盡情地表露自己，非常肯定且感動。沅達用畫冊裡的「系列三：通道」為例，說明自己長期的內在掙扎：門，是要開還是不開？「開門，進來，你真的要想一下，就像爸爸媽媽在小孩面前衝突，他們只想到自己，不會想到孩子，所以繼續打架，我無能為力，只能在旁邊看。」沅達以門來表達自己內在的抉擇，是要往前還是轉身離去？是要面對或者視若無睹？是想嘗試新的可能，或者留在原地？

這孩子面對眼前充滿荊棘的世界，除了驚恐，同時也讓自己有了另一種（或多種）可能。他用「系列五：幸福之路」最後的一幅畫〈笑一笑〉告訴我：「爬山，遇到下雪，你要哭著回家嗎？」人，有權利生氣，可以哭、可以笑，裝笨的他，早已看透大人的世界，「笑笑，就過了。只要活著，就可以選擇開門、關門。」沅達看人生的方式出人意料地早熟，怎會是「笨蛋」？

每一扇門都是一個通道，也都是無限可能。

然而沅達究竟是如何走過痛苦？開門與關門的關鍵為何？因為想更深入他的內心，所以在同一天深夜，我們進行了第二場對話。

夜裡的沅達，很快進入了回憶隧道。他記得爸媽最常掛在嘴邊的話就是「沒錢」「工作很忙」，可是他卻又清楚的知道，這些都是大人的藉口，「他們每天做工，根本都是仆街（廣東話，意指完蛋了），爸爸媽媽不知道我當個笨蛋，是為了等他們。」

兒時的沅達聽見爸爸媽媽衝突，只能哭泣，一路成長以來，內心的脆弱與害怕無處傾訴，沅達只能想辦法麻痺自己的感覺；但越是這樣想，腦子裡的聲音反而越多。後來，一個人的沅達，也不再是一個人，因為內在很多聲音湧現陪伴他，或說，困擾他。

「談談這些聲音？」我問。沅達深深嘆了一口氣後，突然語氣嚴厲，要求在身邊的媽媽離開。

◉場景一：媽媽不在場

沅達這突如其來的動作，讓空氣瞬間凝固。「叫媽媽走，是很痛苦的。」話一說完，沅達換了一個人，雙眼睜得大大，眼神變得銳利憤怒，他像是跟自己對話，而非回應我的採訪。

　　困擾他多年聲音，就是死。24 小時都想死的他，不斷來回交戰：「我跟自己講，你去死啊！死就死啊，沒什麼；但另一個聲音又說，你得活著。」沅達像是在控訴什麼，連珠砲似地直陳內在所想，但他沒有失控，談了約莫十分鐘後，回神了，他把自己整理好，再度請媽媽回到採訪線上。

　　沅達特別叮嚀我：「這事不要放在書裡，讓他們看我，還是一個好孩子，不然別人真的會以為我怎麼了。」

◉ 場景二：倒帶重來──媽媽在場

　　「我一定要在媽媽面前再表達一次。」他說。沅達的父母在他三歲時離婚，雖然不明白大人的決定，也不知道發生什麼事，但他知道從那之後，爸媽關係已不同，世界也不一樣。

　　「我知道，陪我在一起的人，一定是我自己，還有老天爺。老天爺有多種，也有死神，死神跟我在一起好幾年，所以我常會說自殺啊。後來我頭腦安靜了，這些聲音沒了，就整個好了。」雖然談的都是想死的自己，但這次在媽媽面前談，沅達語氣緩和多了，他不想讓媽媽擔心，也不想欺騙媽媽自己沒事，「剛剛我要媽媽離開，就在想要講給媽咪聽嗎？我想，還是要讓媽媽知道。」他認為每個人多少都有過想死的念頭，但是，「如果我用自己的手殺自己，對嗎？」沅達內在的聲音不斷來回辯證，就像不斷穿越每一扇門、每一扇開開關關的門。沅達意識到這段訪談一直在死裡打轉，他斷然的下了指令：「不要被我影響，不要有自殺的想法，不要放棄自己。走，我們去別的地方！」

▨ part 3：7/16(五) 22:30　3 小時 ▨

　　三週後，我們和沅達再次約了專訪，這次爸爸俊鵬也加入。這對沅達來說，是一件大事，也是一個重要的里程碑。出版書冊，不是為了讓讀者認識無師自通電繪的沅達多麼有才華，而是透過書冊出版，再度讓一家三口重新回到家人的愛，也讓長年孤單的沅達回到父母的懷抱，一起面對彼此曾經的艱難。

　　俊鵬在我們面前簡單且含蓄地表示，很高興有這麼多人參與沅達的生命，也讓他對孩子的內心有更深的了解。據說，在視訊之外的俊鵬感動地淚流不止，身為父親能看到兒子成長與蛻變，俊鵬的喜悅難以言喻。系列一的〈痛〉，是雷電交接的雨天。雨天對沅達來說，是很重要的象徵，是一種很深的孤絕，寒意從內心深處湧現，而沅達可以躲在雨的背後哭泣，如此一來，別人就不知道自己在哭，「你可以說下雨啊，或是沙子跑進眼睛啊。」

即使無助的沅達偷偷哭泣，但他始終相信在情緒隧道的盡頭，會有一道白色的光，即便幽微，希望仍在。「很痛，但沒關係，痛就痛，也因為痛，表示我還活著。」沅達這次娓娓道來自己的痛，不再是深淵，而是多了一些溫柔與光明；且他看見父母親離異，痛的不只是孩子，他們自己也很痛。

沅達分享了許多年前一個朋友的故事。在美國的朋友也不斷想尋死，時常拿著手槍頂著自己，扣板機一按下，就是生死一瞬的差別，沅達能理解他，但沒有跟著朋友在裡頭打轉，因為他更想看清楚自己與生命究竟所為何來。

我怕也不怕死⋯⋯我想看進去，就像我畫出的每一幅畫。

透過畫作〈意識的擴張〉與〈從不孤單〉這兩幅畫，沅達想表達就是這種不放棄「活著」背後的思維。人的情緒與感受有很多，你是要選擇哪一種？而當你以

為自己是孤零零的一個人時，抬頭看看星空，就會明白天空繁星燦爛，從不孤單。

第三次採訪中，沅達仍真實自我揭露黑暗面，但也多了不輕言放棄的意志力。一個 18 歲的孩子的成長歷程是這麼衝撞，即使傷痕累累，可是他仍笑笑的告訴我：「24 小時的聲音很累人，但這些不快樂的事，就是要經歷的，人生就像在走隧道，你是要放棄、坐下來，還是繼續走到隧道口，迎接光？」

:::尾聲:::

對於那些曾經霸凌他的老師與同學，可有話想說？

「以前，我用眼睛看他們，他們會很害怕，但是現在這火已經燒得差不多，我一點都不在意他們。我在意的不是身體的強弱，而是我的腦筋是否清楚，這才是支持我繼續往前走的力量。」沅達不斷強調，每個人的痛苦都不同，每個人也都不一樣，重點在於自己如何看世界、看自己，沒有人是完美的，「但你要從日常中學習，才會變得越來越好。」

這是一個 18 歲孩子的成長故事，千瘡百孔的生命歷程，最令人欽佩的無疑是那無限的能力。沅達透過 19 幅畫、19 面鏡子、19 種生命難題（甚至更多），

但他無畏無懼。跟著他，我們也能重新拾回初生之犢
與生俱足的勇氣。

陳心怡

臺大政治系
東吳政研所碩士
資深媒體人、紀錄片導演，現為視界新聞網總編輯

05. Interview

by Chen Hsinyi

Taro Chua, like all youngsters, turned 18 years old in 2021. He likes animation, electronic gaming and computer science. He expressed sincerely without any pretentiousness. In expressing what were deep inside him, he would do whatever he could to let you know and comprehend all of his thoughts.

Years ago, he was being diagnosed with symptom of Social Isolation by a Psychiatrist. This label brought about unimaginable mental impact not only to Taro, but also to his mom Vanessa and dad Alvin; and it was at this juncture that Taro's casual drawings were discovered by the adults. Drawing, has long silently accompanied Taro in his dealing with boredom, helplessness, anger and even his extremely painful and perplexed childhood, it is just that the busy adults have never knew about his secret world.

Since childhood, Taro already had a big question mark towards life. What's the point of living?

Under the encouragement of "Dr Chen", as how Taro addresses Teacher Chen Zhicheng, Taro began to draw and paint his inner world, one after another. He uses his life in search for answers. In bodily pain and heartache, during the silent night, he had experienced thousands of times in extreme pain: What exactly is this child trying to shout out? What does he want to tell the adults?

This was not an easy interview. Besides the language differences, Taro's thinking logic is usually multi-dimensional and parallel at the same time. If you can't catch up, it would be difficult for you to fully understand him. In addition, the intelligence in him drove him to watch adults (like me), to see how adults go about holding a conversation with him. In order to get closer and deeper with Taro, we did three interviews and two of them were held during midnights. It is easier to get more genuine voices from deep within to emerge during night time.

Part 1: 25th June 2021 17:30 – 19:30 (2hours)

When we re-visit our first interview, we realized that it was just an appetizer. Although the interview took 2 hours, most of the time were spent on familiarizing Taro's unique way of expression. Taro was au fait in English and thus requires Vanessa's interpretation and translation to mandarin. Therefore, during the interview, the participation of "mother" was indeed a special kind of "bridge". Vanessa translated our questions and Taro's answers in full authenticity, without any alteration or filtering as a mother.

In numerous occasions, Taro used "stupid" to describe himself and in doing so, he included his mom: "I am stupid, I am a child of a stupid mother". However, when it comes to the companionship of his mother, Taro was fully aware and even asked me: "Do you want to hear about my mom's story? This mother, I can tell her story until she cry, you all will also cry."

Unlike most parents who may find it hard to accept when they hear how their child express themselves to outsiders. Vanessa not only listened attentively, she recognized and was utterly moved by the fact that her child was able to express himself freely and fully.

Taro cited the [The Path] in the third series of his album, as an example to describe his prolong inner struggles: Door, to open or not to open? "Open the door? Come in? You really got to give it a thought; it's like parents fighting in front of the child, the parents will only think about themselves and never for the child. That's why they kept on fighting and I could only helplessly watch by the side."

In facing this thorny world in front of his eyes, this child was terrified, but at the same time, allowed himself to have different possibilities. He cited the last painting [Just Smile] from series five [Happiness Path] and told me: "When you meet snowy weather while mountain climbing, do you cry and go home?" Everyone has the rights to be angry, to cry, or to laugh. Pretending to be stupid, Taro has long seen through the world of the adults. He continued: "We get past after each smile. As long as we are alive, we can choose to open or close the doors." Taro's perspective towards life was unexpectedly mature, so how can he be "stupid"?

❖ Part 2: 25th June 2021 22:00 – 23:30

(1.5hours) ⬛⬛

How exactly did Taro overcome his pain? What is the essence of the open and close doors? In order to get deeper into his inner world, we proceeded on to our second conversation on the same night.

Taro, in the night, speedily went into his memory lane.

He recalled his parents habitual words were "no money", "busy at work", but he knew these were excuses of the adults, "they work everyday, but basically are pok - gai (Cantonese word describing prone onto the streets akin to penniless) , dad and mom have no idea that I pretended to be stupid was for the purpose of waiting for them.

During his childhood, Taro can only cry whenever he heard conflict between his dad and mom. Whilst growing up, Taro has no avenue to address the fragility and fear in his inner world.

Hence, Taro can only think of ways to numb his feelings. But the more in doing so, the more voices came into his mind. In the end, the lonely Taro was no longer alone, because there were emerging voices accompanying him, or rather harassing him.

"Talk about these voices?" I asked.

Taro's voice turned serious after sighing and requested his mom who was beside him to excuse herself.

● Scene 1: Mom was not at scene.

This sudden and unexpected move by Taro froze the air instantly.

"Asking mom to leave, is very painful". At this juncture, Taro seemed to change into another person. His eyes were wide open, the expression in his eyes became incisive and angry. He seemed to be talking to himself rather than responding to our interview.

The voice that has been harassing him for many years is "death". On a 24 hours warring basis: "I tell myself, you go and die, die only, no big deal; but another voice said, you have to keep living". Taro seemed to be accusing about something, firing like a rapid cannon, while describing his most inner thought. But he did not lose control. After about 10 minutes of conversation, Taro regained and recomposed himself and asked for his mom to be back into the interview.

Taro specifically remind me: "Don't put this issue in the book, let them see that I am still a good kid, else people may wonder what had happened to me."

◉ Scene 2: Rewind Retake - Mom at scene

"I must express myself in front of my mom one more time." Taro said.

Taro's parents divorced while he was three years old. Although he cannot understand the adults decision or what happened, but he knew from that moment onwards, the relationship between dad and mom were no longer the same, the world is no longer the same anymore.

"I know, the only person who can accompany me is myself, and also God. There are many types of God, including the God of Death, this God of Death has been with me for years, thus I often say I wanted to kill myself. Subsequently, my mind became quiet, these voices disappeared, everything then became well." Although the conversation was about the self who wanted to die, but in the presence of the mother, Taro's tone was moderated as he does not want to worry the mother, and at the same time does not want to deceive the mother. "I asked my mom to leave just now was because I was procrastinating whether I should let my mom hear it, I guess, we should let my mom knows."

Taro opined that everyone more or less have the thought of dying, but "If I kill myself with my own hands, is it right?" The endless debate of Taro's inner voices is like walking through each and every door, door that opens and closes.

When Taro realize that the conversation was going in circles, he decisively issue an order: "Do not be affected by me, do not have suicidal thoughts, do not give up yourself. Let's go, let's go to some other place!"

▪▪ Part 3: 16th July 2021 (Friday) 22:30 – 01:30 (3 hours) ▪▪

Three weeks later, we had another interview with Taro again, this time involving his dad, Alvin. This is a mega deal for Taro and also an important milestone. The intention behind the publication of the album is not to showcase Taro's natural flair and talent in drawing, but through this publication, a family of three can once again return to the love of a family. This allow the lonely Taro to return to the parents' embracement, and together, they can address the difficulties and hardship each of them had went through for one another.

Alvin humbly expressed his joy and gratitude for the overwhelming participation from so many people in Taro's life journey. At the same time, Alvin was able to gain deeper insights and understanding of Taro's inner world. We later gathered that Alvin was moved to tears when he witness Taro's growing up and transformation. His joy was beyond words.

The setting of [Pain] from series one, resembles a thundering rainy day. Rain, to Taro, is an important emblem, a sign of deep isolation and emergence of coldness from deep within, and Taro can hide and cry in the rain. As such, no one will know he is crying, "You can say is the rain, or sand grains went into the eyes!".

Despite helplessly crying alone, Taro still believe at the end of the emotional tunnel, there is a ray of white light, regardless how dim, hope is still there.

Taro shared a story of his friend from many years ago. This American friend kept wanting to die, and often find himself pointing a handgun to himself; the difference between life and death is just a matter of a pull of the trigger. Taro understood him but did not entangle with this friend, because Taro is more interested in gaining clarity in himself and his life purpose.

"I am afraid but also not afraid of death... I want to look inside, exactly like how I draw each of my drawings. " Taro's tone was full of affirmation. He said that everyone can die at anytime, but did he/she get/achieve what he/she want? Otherwise, why choose to die at this particular point in time? As for those voices that lingered in his mind, Taro opined that, one has to push oneself to the limit, develop and expand capabilities to the limit, one can then break the opposing polarities of the voices, and accepting one's state. Therefore, whenever I felt low, this old friend from the dark will appear. Taro will still ask: "Can I do more? Make myself to live better?"

Taro accurately expressed the meaning behind these two art pieces: [Expansion of Consciousness] and [Never Alone], that is the never give up "living" attitude. We all have emotions and feelings, which one do you want to choose? Whenever you feel being alone, look up at the starry sky, you will then understand that amongst the brilliancy of the countless stars, you are never alone.

In our third interview, Taro continued to disclose his dark side to me truthfully, but this time, his will of "never give up" has intensified. The growing up of this 18 year old child was bumpy and full of scars, but he can still smilingly say to me: "The 24 hours of voices is very tiring, but this kind of unhappiness, is for us to experience, life is like walking a tunnel; Do you want to give up, sit down, or continue the walk till the end of the tunnel and embrace the light?"

⁘ Epilogue ⁘

Do you have anything to say to those teachers or schoolmates who have bullied you?

"I used to use my eyes to stare at them and they will become frightened; but now this fire has more or less subsided and I don't give a damn about them. What I meant is not the strength of the physical body, but the clarity of my thinking; this is the strength that keeps me going."

Taro kept emphasizing that pain differs from person to person, and each person is not the same, the crux is how one view the world, view oneself, no one is perfect, "But you need to keep learning on a daily basis so that you can become better."

This is a growing up story of a 18 year old child, a life journey riddled with scars, and the most admirable part is un-doubtlessly the infinite ability. Although there were 19 paintings, 19 mirrors, 19 life challenges (or even more), Taro was fearless. Follow Taro, we can also regain our native courage in full.

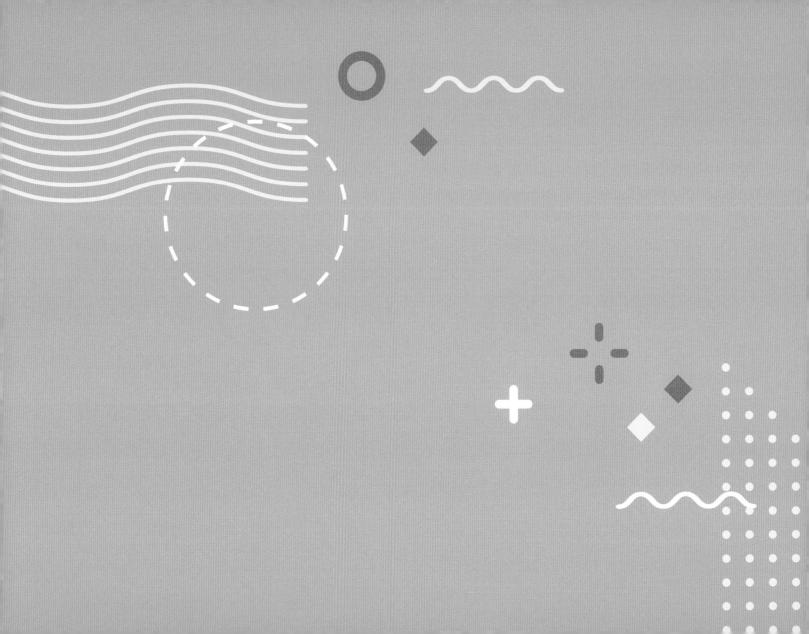

Chapter 2

畫作

ART EXPRESSION

01
痛
Pain

寂靜的雨。一開始是氣氛，但是當進入它的時候，是別的東西。

Rain of Silence. Atmospheric at first but when entered, it's something else.

寂静的雨。一开始是气氛，但是当进入它的时候，是别的东西。

第一次看見這張圖「痛」，讓我看見你內心有說不出的「話」，也就是你內心所有大人無意識給予的傷痛，同時你也無法言說。

When I first saw the Art Expressions, I see the unspoken "Words" in your heart and that was the inexpressible pain given by the adults unconsciously.

第一次看见这张图「痛」，让我看见你内心有说不出的「话」，也就是你内心所有大人无意识给予的伤痛，同时你也无法言说。

導畫與延伸

情緒是看不見的心靈風暴，有時是平靜細雨，有時是風狂雨驟、雷霆閃電。看似巨大的攻擊性裡，有著釋放與再一次新生的力量。

Emotions are invisible psyche storm, sometimes calm and drizzle, sometimes stormy in thunder and lightning. The seemingly huge aggression has the power to release and regenerate again.

情绪是看不见的心灵风暴，有时是平静细雨，有时是风狂雨骤、雷霆闪电。看似巨大的攻击性里，有着释放与再一次新生的力量。

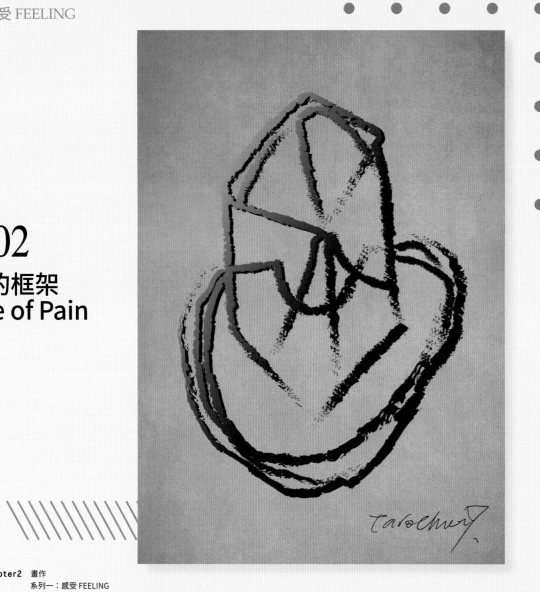

02
痛的框架
Frame of Pain

痛苦的寶石，看透它。你會看到一個反射——你看到誰？
The gem of pain. Look through at it. You'll see a reflection. Who's do you see?
痛苦的宝石，看透它。你会看到一个反射——你看到谁？

你就像一個寶石，本有自身的珍貴，但卻被我們父母、家人、社會等外在的需求和標準所框架了。你的珍貴因此被蒙蔽了，無法躍出你本然的天賦。

You are like a gemstone having your own unique preciousness, but you are restricted by the external demands and standards from parents, family and society. Therefore, your preciousness are hidden, and couldn't exhibit the natural talent in you.

你就像一个宝石，本有自身的珍贵，但却被我们父母、家人、社会等外在的需求和标准所框架了。你的珍贵因此被蒙蔽了，无法跃出你本然的天赋。

導畫與延伸

包裹在幾何切面裡的原礦，有著等待掙脫束縛的靈魂，每一個我都渴望得到解救，破框重生。

The raw ore wrapped in geometrical planes has souls waiting to break free from the shackles of limitations. Every one of "Me" is eager to be rescured and rebirth.

包裹在几何切面里的原矿，有着等待挣脱束缚的灵魂，每一个我都渴望得到解救，破框重生。

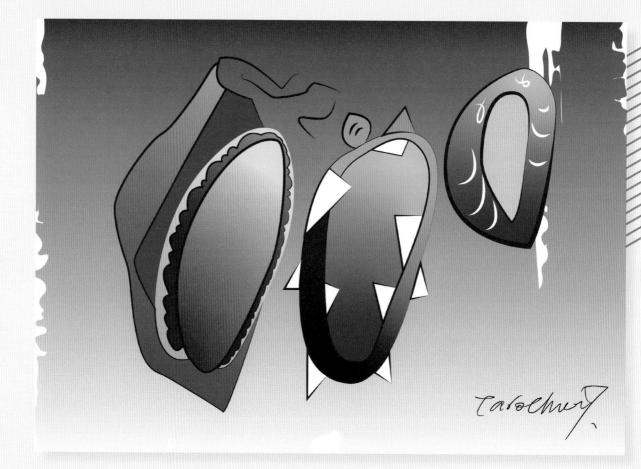

03
風的效應
Tripple Wind

更深入，你把東西放在脖子上。你帶來什麼？你需要什麼？你煩什麼？
Going deeper. You put something on your neck. What do you bring?
What do you need? What do you bother?
更深入，你把东西放在脖子上。你带来什么？你需要什么？你烦什么？

好像風一樣，多希望它能把一切無奈的、不愉快的都吹走……渴望吹走後的平和。

Like the wind, I hope it can blow away all the helplessness and unpleasant... I long for peace after it blows away.

好像风一样，多希望它能把一切无奈的、不愉快的都吹走……渴望吹走后的平和。

導畫與延伸

貼近去感覺，透過肉體感官傳遞的溫度，它回應著心的盼望與失望、煩惱與哀愁，像葉子隨風搖曳、擺盪。

Feeling the warmth through the physical senses that responded to the heart's hopes and disappointments, troubles and sorrows, is like leaves swaying and swinging in the wind.

贴近去感觉，透过肉体感官传递的温度，它回应着心的盼望与失望、烦恼与哀愁，像叶子随风摇曳、摆荡。

04
意識的擴張
Expansion of
Consciouness

膨脹與收縮之間，你看到什麼？
Expanding through thick and thin. What do you see first?
膨胀与收缩之间，你看到什么？

看見你內心不放棄的一句：「我要找出路！」
你的努力所衍生出的多重的面向，是給予大人機會，看見大人的世界究竟是什麼樣。
The never give up words from your heart says: "I want to find a way out! " The multiple aspects derived from your efforts are to give adults the opportunity to see what the adult world is like.
看见你内心不放弃的一句：「我要找出路！」
你的努力所衍生出的多重的面向，是给予大人机会，看见大人的世界究竟是什么样。

導畫與延伸

不斷變化多重面向的自己，強與弱、實與虛、真與假，所有的對立或衝撞、矛盾與掙扎是生命最厚實的韌性（擴張）。
The ever changing multi - faceted self, strong and weak, real and imaginary, true and false, all confrontations or collisions, contradictions and struggles, are life's strongest resilience (expansion).
不斷变化多重面向的自己，强与弱、实与虚、真与假，所有的对立或冲撞、矛盾与挣扎是生命最厚实的韧性（扩张）。

05
存在
Existence

我們的存在是有原因的。沒有理由停止存在。它讓你看見你不是一個人。

We exist for a reason. No reason to cease existence. It's to see that you're not alone.

我们的存在是有原因的。没有理由停止存在。它让你看见你不是一个人。

你用你的存在，讓我感受到我的存在。
You use your existence to let me feel my existence.
你用你的存在，让我感受到我的存在。

導畫與延伸

童真的笑顏與靈動的眼眸是孩子給予我們最珍貴的禮物，也是整日為生活奔忙的大人已遠離的美好。
The innocent smile and smart eyes are the most precious gift that children give us which leaves the adults with a sense of beauty, whenever they leave home for work in their busy life.
童真的笑颜与灵动的眼眸是孩子给予我们最珍贵的礼物，也是整日为生活奔忙的大人已遠離的美好。

06
心碎
Heart Break

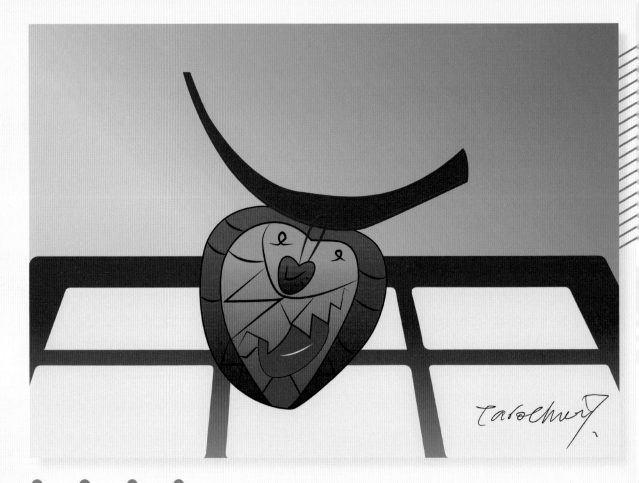

心碎如同小盒墜子。你想打開看見什麼？
Heart Break - "A locket". What do you open to see ?
心碎如同小盒墜子。你想打开看见什么？

每顆心有它的故事，你的心碎是一種象徵，是一個故事引領我願意去愛。
Every heart has its own story. Your broken heart is a symbol. It's a story that guided me to be willing to love.
每颗心有它的故事，你的心碎是一种象征，是一个故事引领我愿意去爱。

導畫與延伸

心碎的感受如同小盒裡需被小心翼翼對待的墜子，傷痕卻是成長蛻變的養分與印記，珍貴而無可取代的經驗。
The feeling of heart break is like a locket needed to be carefully treated. Scars are the nutrients and marks of growth and transformation, precious and irreplaceable experience.
心碎的感受如同小盒里需被小心翼翼对待的坠子，伤痕却是成长蜕变的养分与印记，珍贵而无可取代的经验。

01
虛空
The Void

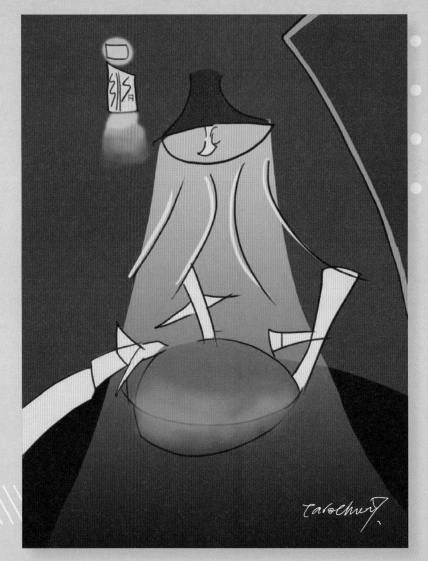

虛空它是空的。
你坐在那裡思考。
你在裡面看到了什麼？
The void is empty. You sit
there and you ponder. What
do you see in it?
虛空它是空的。
你坐在那里思考。
你在里面看到了什么？

心靈家油站（媽媽的話）

生活有許多交叉口，是你讓我看見人生的可能性，而不只是單一性的選擇。因你，我學會了彈性、興起好奇心而推動行動起來。

There are many cross roads in life, but it is you, who have led me to realise its possibilities instead of no alternatives. Because of you, I learned to become flexible and with the push of aroused impetus of curiosity, came action.

生活有许多交叉口，是你让我看见人生的可能性，而不只是单一性的选择。因你，我学会了弹性、兴起好奇心而推动行动起来。

導畫與延伸

我坐在空無一物的靜謐裡，任由許許多多的想法與念頭流過。我在虛空裡，遇見最真實的自己，等待啟航穿越至另一個時空間。

While sitting in the silence of the void, I allow many ideas and thoughts to pass by. In the void, I met my truest self, waiting to take off to another dimension of time and space.

我坐在空无一物的静谧里，任由许许多多的想法与念头流过。我在虚空里，遇见最真实的自己，等待启航穿越至另一个时空间。

01
門（屏障）
Gates

你看到眼前的東西，你不知道它是什麼、它可能是什麼。你有膽量進去嗎？
You see something in front of you, you don't know what it is and what it maybe. Are you brave enough to enter？
你看到眼前的东西，你不知道它是什么、它可能是什么。你有胆量进去吗？

心靈家油站（媽媽的話）

你的掙扎，媽媽看見了。你要有勇氣選擇，媽媽等你去開那扇門……我的孩子，媽媽永遠陪著你！
Mom sees your struggles. Be courageous to make choices, mom shall wait for you to open that door... my child, mom is with you forever!
你的挣扎，妈妈看见了。你要有勇气选择，妈妈等你去开那扇门……我的孩子，妈妈永远陪着你！

導畫與延伸

自我探索是走向內在未知的旅程。黑暗裡，似有若無，分化與恐懼之聲不斷升起，然而，自性始終如同遠處的微光閃耀在前方的道路。
Self exploration is a journey towards the unknown inner self. In all darkness, lies the endless and faint whispers of differentiation and fear. Sense of selfhood remains like a glint in a distant, glimmering the roads ahead.
自我探索是走向内在未知的旅程。黑暗里，似有若无，分化与恐惧之声不断升起，然而，自性始终如同远处的微光闪耀在前方的道路。

02
深入
Deeper

你進去，有一扇門。
You go inside, there's a door.
你进去，有一扇门。

心靈家油站（媽媽的話）

孩子，不要害怕……你看見了，我也看見了。那扇門內還有一道道的門。我們一起加油，勇敢的深入，允許我們彼此能夠再次相信「是可以的！」謝謝你給媽媽機會，允許媽媽認識你。

My child, do not be afraid... You see it, I see it too. There are many doors inside that door. Come on, lets be courageous and firmly believe that [we can]. Thank you for giving mom this opportunity to allow me to know you.

孩子，不要害怕……你看见了，我也看见了。那扇门内还有一道道的门。我们一起加油，勇敢地深入，允许我们彼此能够再次相信「是可以的！」谢谢你给妈妈机会，允许妈妈认识你。

導畫與延伸

我鼓起勇氣向未知尋去，深邃的黑洞儼然是多重時空宇宙。世界仍吵雜紛亂，但前方，卻有一扇門，越發清晰可見。

I gathered my courage to explore the unknown, the depth of the black hole lies the multi universe of time and space. While the world remains noisy and in disarray, there is a door clearly visible to the eyes.

我鼓起勇气向未知寻去，深邃的黑洞俨然是多重时空宇宙。世界仍吵杂纷乱，但前方，却有一扇门，越发清晰可见。

03
開門
Opening

如果，你選擇開門，但有個屏障。有屏障，你還會進去嗎？會被困住？或者不是，或許兩者？

If, you chose to open the door and there's a gate, will you go in even if there's a gate? And be trapped? Or not or maybe both?

如果，你选择开门，但有个屏障。有屏障，你还会进去吗？会被困住？或者不是，或许两者？

感恩！謝謝你讓我進入你的世界。讓我看見了不同的世界觀。

I am grateful! Thank you for letting me into your world. I get to see the difference in worldview.

感恩！谢谢你让我进入你的世界。让我看见了不同的世界观。

導畫與延伸

我已然站在門前，思緒仍舊凌亂不堪，好多的自己在打架。我能跨越重重的阻礙，戰勝自己嗎？我能擊倒心魔，轉化啟動新的可能嗎？

While at the door, my thoughts were still messy, my many selves were fighting. Can I overcome the barriers and conquer myself? Can I strike down the demon in me, to transform and ignite new possibilities?

我已然站在门前，思绪仍旧凌乱不堪，好多的自己在打架。我能跨越重重的阻碍，战胜自己吗？我能击倒心魔，转化启动新的可能吗？

04
通道（路徑）
The Path

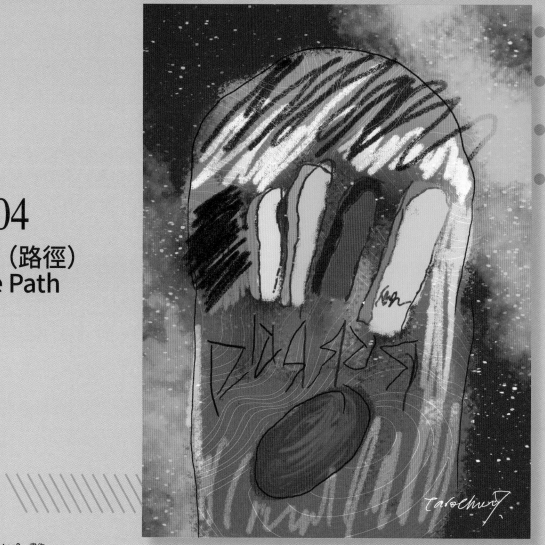

你選擇進入，選擇深入，有四條通道（路徑）——你會去哪裡？

你會選擇什麼？是什麼？幸福？悲傷？又或是平靜或憤怒？

You choose to enter it and choose to go deeper, there's 4 paths - where would you go?

What would you choose? What is it? Happiness? Sadness? Or perhaps a calm mind or anger?

你选择进入，选择深入，有四条信道（路径）——你会去哪里？

你会选择什么？是什么？幸福？悲伤？又或是平静或愤怒？

心靈家油站（媽媽的話）

看見你的過程，我好心疼也很欣慰！人生道路雖然有許多交叉口，但以你的經驗，你一定可以的、可行的。孩子，你真的很棒！媽媽為你而驕傲！

Although it pains me to see what you have went through, but I am gratified at the same time. Life has its crossroads, with your experiences, I am sure you can do it. My child, you are really awesome! Mom is so proud of you!

看见你的过程，我好心疼也很欣慰！人生道路虽然有许多交叉口，但以你的经验，你一定可以的、可行的。孩子，你真的很棒！妈妈为你而骄傲！

導畫與延伸

最深的自己就藏在一道又一道的門後，所有未知的、纏繞的、渾沌的種種，在宇宙浩瀚的銀河裡有最清楚的澈照。無論選擇如何的一條路，我將向著未來前去。

My deepest self hides behind the series of doors. All the unknown, twisting and cloudy matters are clearly reflected on the milky way of the greater universe. Regardless of which road I choose, I will embrace the future.

最深的自己就藏在一道又一道的门后，所有未知的、缠绕的、浑沌的种种，在宇宙浩瀚的银河里有最清楚的澈照。无论选择如何的一条路，我将向着未来前去。

01
眼睛
Eyes

看到這個吊飾了嗎？你看到了什麼？只有你能看到⋯⋯
See this pendant?What do you see? Only you can see...
看到这个吊饰了吗？你看到了什么？只有你能看到⋯⋯

心靈家油站（媽媽的話）

心靈的力量，重新用「心眼」看見心中的那把鎖。
Power of the Soul - new insights to discover the lock in the heart.
心灵的力量，重新用「心眼」看见心中的那把锁。

導畫與延伸

懸吊的墜飾隨處擺盪，目視探尋著心的歸屬。肉眼只能看見最表層的委屈與悲傷，唯有心眼能穿透所有的情緒感受，直達天聽。
Hanging pendant swings at random, seeking a heart of belonging. The physical eyes can only see the superficial wronged and sadness. It is only the insights from the heart that can penetrate through all emotions and feelings to reach the heights of heaven.
悬吊的坠饰随处摆荡，目视探寻着心的归属。肉眼只能看见最表层的委屈与悲伤，唯有心眼能穿透所有的情绪感受，直达天听。

02
敞開的門
The Door of Open

你看你進入。門在這裡，你
要怎麼做？打開？
You see you enter. The door
is here. What do you do?
Open?
你看你进入。门在这里，你要
怎么做？打开？

心靈家油站（媽媽的話）

心靈的力量，重新看見那扇敞開的門後的世界有多美。
Power of the Soul － new view on the beauty of the world through the open door.
心灵的力量，重新看见那扇敞开的门后的世界有多美。

導畫與延伸

內在的生命導引我一步一步觸及底層的自己，我能否下定決心──打開心門、放下偽裝與防衛，容許與接納所有的憤怒與悲傷、所有不夠好的自己？
Inner life progressively guides me to touch the deepest part of myself. Am I determine enough － － to open the door of my heart, lay down all comouflage and defences to allow and accept all anger, sadness and the not good enough of me?
内在的生命导引我一步一步触及底层的自己，我能否下定决心──打开心门、放下伪装与防卫，容许与接纳所有的愤怒与悲伤、所有不够好的自己？

03
悲傷
Sadness

你看到悲傷。何不從悲傷轉身？
You see sadness. Why don't you turn sad around?
你看到悲伤。何不从悲伤转身？

心靈家油站（媽媽的話）

心靈的力量，重新看見那悲傷帶來的推動力和可能性的發展。
Power of the Soul - new realisation of drive and possibilities behind all sadness.
心灵的力量，重新看见那悲伤带来的推动力和可能性的发展。

導畫與延伸

悲傷如同所有的感受，能夠被自然轉化。我們終將可以成長得夠強壯，去安撫、牽引內在裡那個曾經備受驚恐的孩子，重新看見陽光背後陽光的念頭。
Like all feelings, sadness can be naturally transformed. We can ultimately become sufficiently strong to comfort and guide the once fearful inner child, to see hope beyond hope itself.
悲伤如同所有的感受，能够被自然转化。我们终将可以成长得够强壮，去安抚、牵引内在里那个曾经备受惊恐的孩子，重新看见阳光背后阳光的念头。

04
從不孤單
Never Alone

你從不孤單。看到幫助，永不放棄。相信你自己，不要放棄！
You are never alone. See help and never give up. Believe in yourself. DO NOT give up!
你从不孤单。看到帮助，永不放弃。相信你自己，不要放弃！

心靈家油站（媽媽的話）

心靈的力量，重新感受到是被支持的！
Power of the Soul－new sense of being supported!
心灵的力量，重新感受到是被支持的！

導畫與延伸

心的吶喊，我給予自己最堅實的鼓勵，一個簡單深厚的信心，如同宇宙與我一對一的守護關係。生命從不曾被遺落，我們都是最閃耀的一顆星。
My heart screams, and I give myself the most bullish encouragement: one simple yet profound faith, just like how the universe had safeguarded me. Life were never lost, we are all the brightest star.
心的吶喊，我给予自己最坚实的鼓励，一个简单深厚的信心，如同宇宙与我一对一的守护关系。生命从不曾被遗落，我们都是最闪耀的一颗星。

01
童年
Childhood

你的童年，想像所有美好的
時光。
Your very childhood. Imagine
all the good times.
你的童年，想象所有美好的时
光。

心靈的力量，重新的看見及放大美好的時光。
Power of the Soul – new discovery and magnification of good times.
心灵的力量，重新的看见及放大美好的时光。

導畫與延伸

美好快樂的童年裡，有著我對生命最單純的渴望。溜滑梯、盪鞦韆、跳格子……所有孩子的遊戲訴說著無邪的天真、無際的想像、無限的自由。
My simplest desire in life lies amongst the fond happiness of my childhood. All children's games, the slides, swings, hopscotch.... displays the innocence, naive, borderless imaginations and limitless freedom.
美好快乐的童年里，有着我对生命最单纯的渴望。溜滑梯、荡秋千、跳格子……所有孩子的游戏诉说着无邪的天真、无际的想象、无限的自由。

02
諒解
Understanding

沒有人了解另外一個人。何不在多重事情方面裡去了解彼此？
No one understand each other. So why not understand each other in many ways for many things?
沒有人了解另外一个人。何不在多重事情方面里去了解彼此？

心靈家油站（媽媽的話）

心靈的力量，重新以心靈視角去看見、去了解所有的不完美。
Power of the Soul － new insights and understanding of imperfection through psyche perspectives.
心灵的力量，重新以心灵视角去看见、去了解所有的不完美。

導畫與延伸

誤解產生隔閡，我把自己鎖進沒有人理解的世界。開啟心門之鑰需由心去同理與諒解，我願意傾聽、願意溝通、願意表達就是與自己最深的和解。
While misunderstanding produces barriers, I locked myself in a world where no one understands. Empathy and understanding from the heart is the key to unlock the door of the heart. My willingness to listen, communicate and express, are the deepest reconciliation I can have with myself.
误解产生隔阂，我把自己锁进没有人理解的世界。开启心门之钥需由心去同理与谅解，我愿意倾听、愿意沟通、愿意表达就是与自己最深的和解。

03
結論
Conclusion

關於結論。為了快樂，你需要時間。要快樂和結論，帶來一切。
About conclusion. To be happy, you need time. Being happy and in conclusion, brings everything.
关于结论。为了快乐，你需要时间。要快乐和结论，带来一切。

心靈的力量，重新由後見之明看見，所有發生都是最好的安排。
Power of the Soul - new hindsight that all happenings are arranged in it's best form.
心灵的力量，重新由后见之明看见，所有发生都是最好的安排。

導畫與延伸

最終我們會明白生命是享受和體驗快樂的一段漫長過程，唯有容許自己真正成為自己，才能實質的貢獻與成就。
Ultimately, we get to understand that life is a long process of indulging and experiencing of happiness. Only through allowing myself to be truely myself, can I be of real contributions and accomplishments.
最终我们会明白生命是享受和体验快乐的一段漫长过程，唯有容许自己真正成为自己，才能实质的贡献与成就。

04
笑一笑
Just Smile

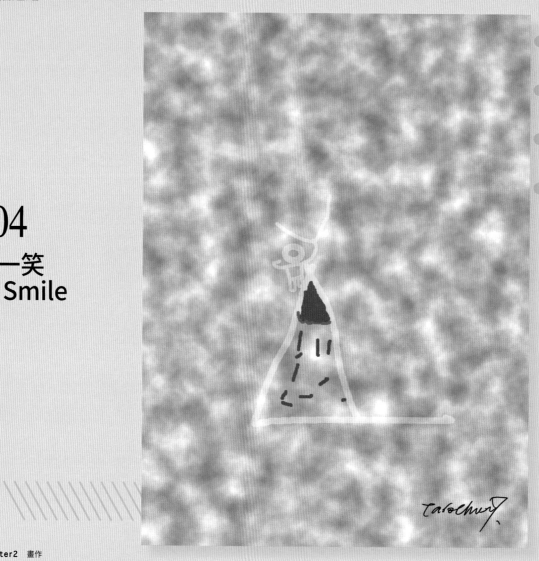

笑一笑，要開心、要感恩，永不放棄。微笑以對，艱難選擇人（艱難給人考驗）。走自己的路，不要迷路，好就會更好。

Just smile. Be happy. Be grateful. Never give up and smile through. Bad times choose people. Right and more right. Follow your own path. Don't Stray.

笑一笑，要开心、要感恩，永不放弃。微笑以对，艰难选择人（艰难给人考验）。走自己的路，不要迷路，好就会更好。

心靈的力量，重新忠實且誠正的做自己，以幽默風趣對待一切。
Power of the Soul － new loyalty and honesty of being true to yourself, and treat everything with a sense of humour.
心灵的力量，重新忠实且诚正的做自己，以幽默风趣对待一切。

導畫與延伸

生命充滿活力與無限可能，一路上，我為自己設定了不同關卡與挑戰。我就像登山的健將，不斷攻頂與突破。笑一笑吧！你也能再找到力量向前！
Life is full of vitality and infinite possibilities and along the way, I set up hurdles and challenges. I am like a mountain climber, constantly breaking through myself and reaching for the summit. Smile! You surely can discover the strength to move forward!
生命充满活力与无限可能，一路上，我为自己设定了不同关卡与挑战。我就像登山的健将，不断攻顶与突破。笑一笑吧！你也能再找到力量向前！

Chapter 3

後記
EPILOGUE

01

沅達小語

「我想說的就是──好好享受生活。」

給讀者：

我只是一個來自任何地方的普通人，沒有什麼新鮮，不是來炫耀什麼的……只是在這裡告訴你：要活著，最重要的是享受生活。

書的內容已經說了需要說的。

如果你問我：「為了在生活中找到答案並快樂的生活──經歷它。」

01. Taro Chua's words

"I want to say is just live life and enjoy it"

To the readers:

I am just a normal average guy from anywhere, nothing new, not here to show off or anything… Just here to tell you to live life and enjoy it most of all yeah.

The book content has said what it needs to be said.

If you were to ask me, "in order to find answers in life and to live happily - Live through it"

02

爸爸的祝福

孩子，你真的很棒！爸爸永遠陪伴你……

此畫作讓身為父親的我非常感動和無比的欣慰！透過整個過程，我也更了解孩子的壓力和他的經歷。沅達能夠自我消化、自我整合、自我療癒，是一件非常不容易的事。沅達能有這麼棒的勇氣去主觀表達出自己的感受，同時藉以此畫作也能夠讓更多人了解一個孩子的內心感受與生活的看法，實在是了不起。沅達對事物和生命有他獨特的見解，使得我很放心了。我的孩子，沅達，他的勇氣和其他人不一樣，而且要強大的多！

我為我的孩子，沅達，感到非常的驕傲……他不僅幫助了我們，也能透過他的畫作去幫助更多的孩子和不同的家庭。

衷心感謝蘇馬利體集團協助出版此畫冊，也感謝 Dr. Chen 的用心陪伴及發掘了我的孩子的潛能……

我想跟沅達說：「孩子，你真的很棒！爸爸永遠陪伴你……」

02. Blessings from Taro's dad

My child, you are really great! Dad will always be with you…

Being a father, I am very touched and pleased with this Art Expression Album! Through the album's production process, it allows me to better understand about my child's stress and his experiences. Taro's ability to digest, manage, integration and self-healing is truly remarkable. He is brave and courageous to express his feelings subjectively, and concurrently through his Art Expression Album, allows more people to understand a child's inner feelings and views on life. This is really amazing.

Taro has his unique insights on things and life, which makes me feel relieved. My child, Taro, his courage is different from others because he is so much stronger!

I am very proud of my child, Taro. Taro's Art Expression Album, not only helped us, but he could also help many more children and different families.

I sincerely thank Sumari Group for their assistance in publishing his Art Expression Album, and I also thank Dr Chen for his dedicated companionship and uncovered my child's potentials.

I want to say to Taro: "My child, you are my best! Dad will always be with you..."

國家圖書館出版品預行編目資料

爸爸媽媽，請你看見我！／蔡沅達 著．
 -- 初版 . -- 臺北市：圓神出版社有限公司，2021.11
80 面；23×17 公分 . -- （圓神文叢；305）
ISBN 978 - 986 - 133 - 795 - 1（平裝）
1. 心理治療 2. 繪畫治療

178.8   110014977

www.booklife.com.tw   reader@mail.eurasian.com.tw

 305

爸爸媽媽，請你看見我！

作　　　者／蔡沅達
採訪撰文／陳心怡
總 指 導／陳志成
審　　議／朱瓊英‧傅美玲‧施莉莉
英譯人員／洪于喬‧郭素珍‧郭素玉‧林恩維
專案負責／呂佳佳
發 行 人／簡志忠
出 版 者／圓神出版社有限公司
地　　址／臺北市南京東路四段50號6樓之1
電　　話／（02）2579 - 6600‧2579 - 8800‧2570 - 3939
傳　　真／（02）2579 - 0338‧2577 - 3220‧2570 - 3636
總 編 輯／陳秋月
主　　編／賴真真
專案企畫／賴真真
責任編輯／歐玟秀
校　　對／歐玟秀‧吳靜怡
美術編輯／簡　瑄
行銷企畫／陳禹伶‧朱智琳
印務統籌／劉鳳剛‧高榮祥
監　　印／高榮祥
排　　版／陳采淇
經 銷 商／叩應股份有限公司
郵撥帳號／18707239
法律顧問／圓神出版事業機構法律顧問　蕭雄淋律師
印　　刷／國碩印前科技股份有限公司
2021年11月　初版
※ 誠摯感謝英譯人員協助翻譯作業

定價 300 元 　　　　ISBN 978-986-133-795-1